AN INTEREST-BASED MEDIATION
MEDIATOR-TRAINEE AND STUDENT HANDBOOK

By

Melinda J. Branscomb
Associate Professor
Seattle University School of Law

and

Sue Ann Allen
Training Director
Dispute Resolution Center of King County

SEATTLE
UNIVERSITY
SCHOOL OF LAW

DisputeResolution
CENTER *of* KING COUNTY

MELINDA J. BRANSCOMB & SUE ANN ALLEN, AN INTEREST-BASED MEDIATION — MEDIATOR-TRAINEE AND STUDENT HANDBOOK (2010) (www.MediationTrainingResources.com).

ISBN-10: 1453628533.
ISBN-13: 9781453628539.

Written, produced, and directed by

Melinda J. Branscomb, Associate Professor, Seattle University School of Law and

Sue Ann Allen, Training Director, Dispute Resolution Center of King County

The DVD (92 min.) that this MEDIATOR-TRAINEE AND STUDENT HANDBOOK is designed to supplement is:

> AN INTEREST-BASED MEDIATION: FROM WORKPLACE DISPUTE AND DISCHARGE TO ACCOMMODATION AND AGREEMENT - A NARRATED MEDIATOR-TRAINING VIDEO (Melinda J. Branscomb & Sue Ann Allen, 2010) (DVD, www.MediationTrainingResources.com).

The hypothetical facts center on a former employee and her supervisor mediating issues surrounding the employee's allegedly-unlawful discharge. The video demonstrates the interest-based, facilitative mediation style, as the mediator works directly with the parties to create solutions that meet their underlying interests. The mediator is Andrew Kidde, J.D., Program Manager of the Bellevue Neighborhood Mediation Program, Bellevue, WA.

Table of Contents

Learning Objectives 3

Background about Mediator Styles and Approaches 5

Introduction 12

Description of Scenario 14

Stage I: Mediator's Opening Statement 16

Stage II: Parties' Opening Statements and Mediator Paraphrase 18

Stage III: Agenda 20

Stage IV: Negotiations 24

Caucus 26

Stage V: Resolution and Closure 28

About the Producers 31

Special Thanks 33

About the Mediator 33

Post Script Regarding Multiple Sclerosis 35

Caucus Exercise

Instructions 37

Exercise 39

Learning Objectives

This video demonstrates how mediators can . . .

1. achieve process control while creating a party-centered process

2. write an appropriate mediation agenda

3. use the agenda effectively

4. focus on underlying interests, rather than on positions about who is right and wrong, and rather than solely focusing on the law

5. shift parties from rehashing the past to working towards resolution

6. create movement with positional parties

7. restore broken relationships

8. empower parties to negotiate effectively for themselves

9. intervene appropriately when parties ...

   - have heated exchanges
   - refuse to discuss topics
   - get in attack-and-defend cycles
   - push other party's "hot buttons"
   - interrupt
   - blame and accuse

Background about Mediator Styles and Approaches

In the seminal book, GETTING TO YES, Fisher and Ury espoused the advantages of interest-based negotiations.[1] Hallmarks of interest-based bargaining include separating one's feelings about the opposing negotiator from the issue being negotiated ("soft on the people, hard on the problem"[2])*,* negotiating with an eye towards *mutual* gain, and negotiating based on what each party truly needs -- the *underlying interests* that motivate them to assert the positions they take -- rather than simply arguing about which of the negotiators' respective fixed proposals should be adopted.

By focusing on underlying interests, it may be that the negotiators discover creative options that they had not previously considered. Also, they may discover multiple outcomes that could solve the problem satisfactorily for both parties, as opposed to the limited win/lose solution that occurs when each negotiator rigidly insists on his or her position.

In the example of two spouses arguing over where to take a winter vacation, Harold may insist that they should go to the Mexican coast, while Annette may be adamant that they should go to Washington, D.C. The spouses are stuck in the either-or dilemma of position-based bargaining. Perhaps they will "compromise," or split the difference. They could spend half of their vacation in each locale. Alternatively, they could compromise by going to Mexico this winter and to the Capital next summer. Compromise is a useful resolution tool. However, with compromise both parties get some of their goals met, but not all. Each ends up partly unsatisfied.

By contrast, if our couple uses interest-based bargaining, they will seek to learn about the reasons for their respective positions. Perhaps Annette wanted to visit the museums in the nation's Capital. Perhaps Harold preferred Mexico because he likes the natural beauty of the coast and likes exploring different cultures. Discussing these respective preferences, the couple may decide to go neither to Mexico nor to the Capital. Perhaps they will visit the Olympic Peninsula on the west coast. There, they can explore beautiful beaches, and they can learn interesting history lessons at

---

1 R. Fisher et al, GETTING TO YES: NEGOTIATING AGREEMENT WITHOUT GIVING IN (New York: Penguin Books, 2d ed.1991).

2 *Id* at 10, 17, 20-22.

several Native American museums, experiencing a culture different from theirs. They can fully satisfy all of their respective needs and goals.

If we dig deeply enough, we find that Annette's and Harold's interests are universal in nature. Annette's goal of going to a museum may stem, for example, from a deeper underlying interest in achieving intellectual satisfaction (in this case, by learning about history), or in achieving respect and status (due to her knowledge of history). Harold's goal of going to the coast may stem from underlying aesthetic interests (seeing beautiful scenery), leisure interests (relaxing on the beach), or physical interests (exercising by walking on the beach). His goal of experiencing another culture may stem from artistic interests (he loves music of other countries), or from intellectual interests (he likes learning about different peoples). Interests are universal in that people around the world are motivated by intellectual satisfaction, aesthetics, leisure, physical expression, artistic appreciation, respect, status, and so forth.

That said, different cultures and different people express their interests differently. For example, different activities may be considered "leisure" in different countries. In fact, what looks like "leisure" to one person (reading a long, dense novel) may be exhausting to another. Also, different individuals may prioritize the same interests differently. Annette isn't really wild about music, although Harold is. Perhaps she enjoys the visual arts.

The most fundamental and powerful interests stem from the most basic of human needs, such as physical safety, security, fairness, respect, or autonomy. Interests can be grouped into categories, such as economic interests; moral and psychological interests (integrity, self-respect, peace of mind, etc.); ego or psychic interests (accomplishments, autonomy, etc.); influence interests (reputation, credibility, etc.); ideological interests (values and beliefs); social or relational interests; and the like.[3]

Despite the critical importance of underlying interests to all individuals in conflict, when a legal dispute has crystallized,[4] and attorneys begin discussing the case with clients and "opposing" counsel, they can quickly fall into fixed positions based on each side's

---

3   *From* Douglas N. Frenkel & James H. Start, The Practice of Mediation, 35 (Aspen Publishers 2008) (slightly modifying list of Goodpaster, 95-96).

4   We refer here to cases that are in litigation or in which litigation is contemplated, as contrasted with planning, transactional negotiations, and other such pre-dispute legal negotiations and advice.

assessment of who is right and who is wrong under the law. Critics have noted a "pinched perspective" that particularly dominates settlement discussions of cases that are in the litigation stream,[5] as advocates often get caught up arguing solely about their differently-perceived clients' legal entitlements and legal obligations. Yet, it may be that various other outcomes -- outcomes based on satisfying the clients' respective underlying needs, interests, and goals -- could satisfy the clients equally well or better than the limited outcomes that the law affords or that a judge or jury is allowed to award.[6]

For example, in a positional negotiation of an employment discharge, a rights-based focus would center primarily on whether the discharge was legal, and if not, how much the employer will pay. Interest-based bargaining might include a range of additional negotiation topics, such as:

- possible steps to protect the reputational interests of both the employee and the employer

- payment of additional benefits to the employee, or even a portion of the settlement sum to a charity of the employee's choice

- preventative steps the company will take to avoid similar situations in the future, such as staff training or closer supervision

- implementation of grievance procedures employees may use if discipline or discharge is imminent or has occurred, which may avert the need for litigation

- implementation of remedial or disciplinary steps to which supervisors may refer future "problem" employees, which may avert the need for discharge

- possible reinstatement to the job or a different job

---

5 Leonard L. Riskin & Nancy A. Welsh, *Is That All There Is?: "The Problem" in Court-oriented Mediation,* 15 Geo.Mason L.Rev. 863, 863 (2008).

6 Three important factors are virtually irrelevant at trial: The law focuses not on relationships, but on rules. It focuses not on people's interests, but on their rights. It looks not to the future, but to the past (non-injunction settings). One predicament that is *not* inherent in litigation, however, is that along the course of representation, settlement negotiations, or mediation, advocates and attorney-mediators can narrow the focus to money when other solutions in addition to (or occasionally in lieu of) money might resolve the problems equally well or better from the client's perspective. *See generally, e.g., id.;* James J. Alfini, *Trashing, Hashing, and Bashing it Out: Is This the End of "Good Mediation"?,* 19 Fla. St. U. L.Rev. 47, 66-71 (1991); Dwight Golann, Mediating Legal Disputes: Effective Strategies for Neutrals and Advocates, 227 (ABA Publishing, 2009)("lawyers have seen mediation simply as a method of facilitating traditional bargaining over money .... Some lawyers still favor this approach, but it does not take full advantage of what a mediator can do.").

- how to address any inter-personal issues that are important for reinstatement to be successful

- assisting the employee in developing additional skills through retraining

- assisting the employee in finding another job

- what information the employer and/or employee will communicate to other employees about the situation

- what information the parties will communicate to the press

- content of employee's official work record

- apologies by one or both sides

- enhanced understanding of – and more importantly, addressing and potentially alleviating -- the negative emotional impacts of the dispute on one or both sides.[7]

- content of future recommendation letters regarding the employee.[8]

Scholars and other critics express concern that the decision to approach problems narrowly in mediation not only forecloses deliberation of such far-ranging issues

---

7 Research indicates that attorneys have a tendency to minimize the emotional and interpersonal aspects of disputes when negotiating settlements. *See, e.g.,* Joshua D. Rosenberg, *Interpersonal Dynamics: Helping Lawyers Learn the Skills, and the Importance, of Human Relationships in the Practice of Law,* 58 U.Miami L.Rev. 1225, 1229 (2004)("most lawyers and academics vastly overestimate the importance of reason and logic" in solving clients' problems); *Id.,* at 1230 fn.22 (citing research concluding that "the single greatest weakness of most negotiators is that they too often fail to even *consider* the thinking and emotions of others"); Vernellia R. Randall, *The Myers-Briggs Type Indicator, First Year Law Students and Performance,* 26 Cumb.L.Rev. 63, 92 (1995-96); Riskin, *et al, supra* note 5, at 889 and research discussed therein; David A. Hyman, *When and Why Lawyers are the Problem,* 57 DePaul L.Rev. 267, 275 (2008)(noting that lawyers are encouraged to be "dispassionate" and "to leave their personal feelings at home," and citing findings that they score low in "intimacy skills and sociability"). Yet, in negotiations a great deal can be accomplished by "allowing the parties to talk about their feelings and disagreements in a controlled setting." Golann, *supra* note 6, at 7. Indeed, frequently it is only after the parties have had a chance to vent their feelings – in a *managed* environment that keeps communication civil enough to be productive – that they are ready and willing to consider reasonable settlement proposals or to work together towards comprehensive solutions that can deliver on the potential of mediation to meet a broad range of underlying interests. *See id.* at 4-7.

8 This list was adapted in large part from Nancy Maisano, *Expanding the Pie in Employment Mediations,* 28 Bar Bulletin 7 (King Co. Bar Assoc., Sept. 2009)(discussing benefits of including non-monetary and creative options in employment mediations).

and interests, but that in the case of attorney negotiators, it is "rarely the result of deliberation or even consultation that includes clients."[9]

Of course there can be valid reasons for negotiators to choose a rights-based focus or for limiting the topics of a negotiation solely to an exchange of money. Sometimes the only issue *is* who is right, and sometimes the dispute *is,* indeed, only about money. The concern is not a question of those options' legitimacy, but of a tendency for lawyers automatically – that is, non-critically – to default to a rights-based and primarily financial focus where interest-based bargaining might have better served the clients' interests.[10]

---

9   Riskin, *et al, supra* note 5, at 896-97 (fn. omitted). Riskin and Welsh report that "[t]he repeat players tend to assume implicitly that the problem definition is narrow; this leads them to establish procedures that will be limited primarily to the kind of information that is relevant to litigation (and economic) issues.... [I]nformation and perspectives that would broaden the focus are largely excluded, absent, or marginalized." *Id.,* 896-97, *fn. omitted. See also* Rosenberg, supra note 7, at 1220 fn.2 (2004)(noting that "law students learn well how to review what has happened, to assign blame, and to argue persuasively about why one party ought to be held responsible for what has gone wrong," as opposed to learning "creative and forward-looking problem solving, with an emphasis on identifying and working to pursue each party's interests and goals."); Golann, *supra* note 6, at 52-58 (offering mediators suggestions for how to help -- or persuade -- advocates to shift from rights to interests); James J. Alfini, *Mediation as a Calling: Addressing the Disconnect Between Mediation Ethics and the Practices of Lawyer Mediators,* 49 S.Tex. L.Rev. 829, 833-35 (2008) ("disconnect" between mediator-ethics and mediation as practiced by some attorneys); Carol J. Brown, *Facilitative Mediation: The Classic Approach Retains Its Appeal,* Mediate. com (2002) (www.mediate.com/articles/brownC.cfm) (explaining preference for facilitative mediation model). One lawyer recounts her experience: *"My first custody trial went well from the adversarial legal perspective – that is, my client won custody of the child. I enjoyed the competition of the battle and was pleased at the result, at first. Soon I saw that winning was not the end of the case. My client, her ex-husband, and their son remained embroiled in conflict. They were all miserable and fought about every little thing ... The trial had failed to bring the peace that was needed for them to move forward. Not long after that, I 'won' another custody case. Again, the 'game' of the competition was exhilarating. I did everything I'd learned to do in law school. After the trial, my client, an extremely dedicated mother, told me that she would give up custody of her children before she would ever go through another trial."* The author then began to look for alternatives to such a practice. J. Kim Wright, LAWYERS AS PEACEMAKERS, XXVI-XXVII (ABA 2010).

10 The reasons for such an automatic default include (1) the traditional litigation-focused, and therefore rights-focused, law school curriculum that does not adequately expose law students to negotiation theory, complex problem solving, and other dispute resolution skills (*see* Leonard L Riskin, *Mediation and Lawyers,* 43 Oh.St. L.J. 29, 43-48, 57-59 (1982); (2) the ad hoc development of the mediation profession without uniform standards to ensure mediators are trained in the full range of styles, and a resulting dearth of mediators who are

The conceptual distinction between an interest-based approach to negotiations and a narrower, positional approach was applied specifically to the mediation context by Leonard Riskin in his now well-known "grid."[11] Riskin describes four basic mediator orientations. One axis of the grid, pertaining to how mediators view the problem at hand, explains that mediators range from defining the dispute narrowly (a positional, legalistic perspective) to defining it broadly (an interest-based perspective). A second axis, pertaining to how mediators view their own role, illustrates that they range from facilitating the process, on the one hand, to evaluating what the substantive outcome should be, on the other.

The DVD, *"An Interest-based Mediation..."* highlights an interest-based focus in an attempt to engage in broad problem-solving, rather than focusing on right-wrong positions. The mediator uses a facilitative style rather than a highly directive or substantively evaluative one.[12]

---

able to address the intangible aspects of disputes; (3) a "litigation mindset" of attorneys shaped by courtroom advocacy for the limited outcomes that judges and juries can award; (4) the large number of judges who entered the mediation field after lifelong careers centering on rights to the exclusion of interests (5) lawyers' familiarity with judicial settlement conferences, which are rights-based; (6) institutionalization and court-annexation of mediation services; (7) lack of training and skill in understanding the full dimensions of clients' "problems" as defined from the clients' perspectives; (8) attorney and mediator lack of training and skill in managing client emotions; (9) time constraints that push negotiators to "get right to the numbers"; (10) assumptions that money is the way, or the sole way, to address and solve problems; (11) competitiveness and distrust between attorney-negotiators; (12) attorneys' psychological makeup (see supra note 7); (13) habit and inertia; and (14) the fact that "creative" solutions do not cover attorney's fees.

11 Leonard L. Riskin, *Mediator Orientations, Strategies, and Techniques: A Grid for the Perplexed*, 1 HARVARD NEGOTIATION L.REV. 7-51 (1996); Leonard L. Riskin, *Mediator Orientations, Strategies and Techniques*, 29 ALTERNATIVES TO THE HIGH COST OF LITIGATION, Sept., 1994, at 111; *revisited in* Leonard L. Riskin, *Replacing the Mediator Orientation Grids, Again: Proposing a 'New New' Grid System*, 29 ALTERNATIVES TO THE HIGH COST OF LITIGATION 127-32 (Sept. 2005) and articles cited therein.

12 As stated in the film, the authors do not purport to assert that this is the "only," or always "best" mediation model, as there is not one "right" model for all situations. We do hope that we have achieved our goal of providing an excellent demonstration of this model.

Introduction

Mediation is a confidential dispute resolution process where an impartial mediator helps parties work through their conflict to reach a voluntary solution.

There are several different mediation styles. The style that we teach is facilitative and interest-based. We believe it's one of the most successful methods of resolving disputes because the parties direct the outcome.

Facilitative mediators assist parties in coming up with their own solutions. They don't tell the parties who's right and wrong or what they should do. People who create their own solutions buy in to the outcome, and so they are more likely to comply with agreements.

Our model is also interest-based. This means the mediator focuses broadly on the unmet needs that are driving the conflict. The process is more about meeting underlying interests than deciding who's right and wrong. The parties may see their legal rights as relevant, but this process is less about fixed positions and the past, and more about working together to move forward. Interest-based mediation has the potential for more creative solutions than the win / lose outcomes that evaluative mediators, judges, or juries can order.

Sometimes mediations are conducted entirely in separate rooms, with the mediator shuttling between them, such as when there are insurmountable power imbalances like a history of violence. A full description of shuttle mediation is outside the scope of this video, so let's turn to the advantages of the facilitative, interest-based style.

- It increases communication.

- Meeting jointly provides a chance to correct misunderstandings and deepen empathy.

- It teaches people to advocate for themselves, and to work together.

- It increases trust, because parties don't have to worry about what's said behind closed doors.

- Last, it fosters independence, since the outcome doesn't depend on an outside decision-maker

Facilitative, not directive or evaluative

- **parties fashion solutions**
- **parties "buy in"**
- **parties comply**

Broad View of Problem: underlying interests

- **needs-based, not rights-based**
- **solution-focused, not law-focused**
- **future-oriented, not past-oriented**
- **creative, not limited**

Description of Scenario [13]

This mediation involves the termination of an employee named Sherri from a hypothetical home improvement store. Sherri had done her job well for years, but in recent months she had become tired and forgetful, and her work performance declined. With no explanation for Sherri's erratic behavior, her supervisor, Jean, finally fired Sherri.

After her discharge, Sherri was diagnosed with multiple sclerosis (MS) which, when untreated, explains her symptoms. Sherri filed a lawsuit. However, when she was working neither Sherri nor her boss had considered her to have a "disability," so you may assume that whether the law was violated is not clear. There would be a risk for both Sherri and the company if the case went to trial.[14]

By the time of the mediation, most of Sherri's symptoms are successfully controlled with medication, and her other symptoms may not prevent her from working if some reasonable accommodations can be made. However, returning to work would require repair of the relationship between Sherri and her boss, so the attorneys suggested mediation. The lawyers will be available by telephone during the mediation if needed, and they will review the final settlement.

---

13 The simulation is based on an actual conflict, though the parties' names and type of workplace are fictional. The "actor" portrayed in the video has been negotiating the ups and downs of multiple sclerosis for over a decade, with various levels of accommodations from employers. The individuals in the film are not professional actors. While the roles and topics of the dispute were planned, in order to achieve realism, freshness, and authenticity, neither the lines of the parties nor the lines of the mediator were scripted; the mediation and the pre- and post-mediation interviews are entirely spontaneous.

14 A person with a "disability" is generally defined under federal law as someone with a physical or mental "impairment" that substantially limits a major life activity; who has a "record of" such an impairment, or who is "regarded as" having such an impairment. The employer must provide "reasonable accommodations" for the employee if such accommodations would enable him or her to perform the "essential functions" of the job. The duty to accommodate, however, generally is triggered by the employee putting the employer on notice of the disability and need for accommodations, except where the employer is essentially already on notice because the disability and need are obvious. *See, e.g. Jovanovic v. In-Sink-Erator Div. of Emerson Elec. Co.,* 201 F.3d 894, 899 (7th Cir.2000); EEOC v. Cast Products, Inc., 49 Daily Lab. Rep. (BNA) at A-8 (March 17, 2009); Enica v. Principi, 544 F3d 328 (1st Cir. 2008); Wallin v. Minnesota Dep't of Corrections 153 F.3d 681 (8th Cir. 1998); 29 C.F.R. § 1630.9 and APPENDIX TO PART 1630 (INTERPRETIVE GUIDANCE ON TITLE I OF THE AMERICANS WITH DISABILITIES ACT).

Stage I: Mediator's Opening Statement

The first stage of mediation is the mediator's Opening Statement. It sets the tone, modeling respectful communications, building rapport and trust. The mediator deals with logistics, such as

- how the parties would like to be addressed,
- time constraints,
- whether any court orders are involved,
- whether there are unforeseen conflicts of interest, and
- whether all necessary parties are at the table.

The mediator explains the process, the ground rules or expectations, the roles of the mediator and the parties, and confidentiality, getting buy in from the participants on each of these points. Last, the mediator and parties sign the Agreement to Mediate.

Mediator's Opening Statement

1. Tone, respect, rapport
2. Logistics
3. Process
4. Ground rules
5. Roles
6. Confidentiality
7. Party buy-in
8. Agreement to Mediate

Stage II: Parties' Opening Statements and Mediator Paraphrase

The parties explain the conflict from their differing perspectives. Those opening statements give them uninterrupted time to tell their story. They often need to vent strong feelings. It is important that parties be given the time they need for opening comments. To new mediators this may feel "inefficient," like time is being wasted rehashing the past, but this is the one time in the process where the parties have the opportunity to talk about the past. It's only when the parties have explained their version of what happened and feel understood that they are able to move forward and focus on future solutions.

After each party describes the story from her perspective, the mediator paraphrases those comments. In this way, the mediator makes sure he understands both the content (the facts as the party sees them), and the feelings expressed. When the mediator shows this understanding, the speaker knows she's been heard. The speaker's emotions and perspective are also validated, although the mediator does not necessarily "buy in" to the factual accuracy of what is said. The mediator also reframes inflammatory language to be more neutral. Sometimes the mediator's summary of a party's perspective is the first time the other side truly hears that perspective.

Stage III: Agenda

The agenda is a list of topics to discuss. The topics are the issues, not proposed solutions. The agenda can include non-legal items like communication, relationship, and trust. It lets the parties focus on something neutral, something shared, rather than on their disagreements. It creates agreement on what needs to be discussed. It provides forward momentum, helping keep the conversation focused, structuring the discussion and tracking what has been and remains to be decided. It also provides a visual record of accomplishments as items are "checked off" in negotiations. The items can be discussed in any order. Often parties will start first with a large topic that's difficult but essential. Other times, momentum can be achieved by starting with a smaller item on which agreement is more readily reached.

Agenda: *content, goals, uses*

1. Agreed topics, not proposed solutions
2. Both legal and non-legal items
3. Stated neutrally
4. Momentum
5. Focus
6. Structure and tracking
7. Record of accomplishments

Jean's and Sherri's Agenda

1. **Reasons for Sherri's behavior change**
2. **Education for staff**
3. **Scope of job responsibilities**
4. **Medical issues**
5. **Reasons for, and future of, the lawsuit[15]**
6. **Organization and tracking of tasks**
7. **Assistive technology**
8. **Release time[16]**

---

15 In context, the dialogue in the film makes clear that when Jean asks about "reasons for the lawsuit," she does not mean the *legal* grounds for the suit (which she feels is baseless in any event), but rather why her mentee of over 10 years chose to sue without coming to her first to talk over the situation. While a basic fact pattern was given to the individuals playing "Jean" and "Sherri," the film was not scripted and this dialogue was not planned. Nonetheless, the discussions regarding the lawsuit likely mirror fairly accurately the feelings of hurt and betrayal that a manager such as Jean might experience upon learning that a long-time friend and subordinate had not talked with her about a serious medical condition, or about an intention to hire a lawyer and pursue litigation.

16 You may assume that the lawyers have agreed in advance on the amount of back pay owing, should the parties reach resolution of the more contentious issues in the dispute, and should they negotiate an agreement involving Sherri's reinstatement. Thus, back pay is not on the negotiating agenda.

Stage IV: Negotiations

Facilitating negotiations is where the real art of mediation comes in. The goal is to help the disputants clarify their feelings, identify their interests and needs, consider the impacts of their choices, and help them generate multiple possible solutions that may successfully address everyone's interests. A variety of mediator techniques can serve that end, including focusing the parties and clarifying their positions and proposals by asking open-ended questions and paraphrasing; reframing hostile or accusatory language; tracking & summarizing agreements; reality testing; and the use of silence. When parties are talking to each other productively, the mediator can sit back and observe. If the mediator has successfully set the stage earlier in the process for the parties to work together, then the mediator may have less work to do during negotiations![17]

The parties have negotiated several items[18] and now discuss begin to discuss the lawsuit.[19] The mediator's interventions during this part of the negotiations create the possibility for mutual understanding and empathy. Notice the mediator's effective use of silence to allow important points to sink in.

---

17 As Professor Dwight Golann puts it, "Give parties the initiative," because "as long as the process is moving forward, you can step back and let the parties do the work." Golann, *supra* note 6, at 52.

18 Notice that while the Mediator may have in mind some possible solutions or directions in which the parties could move, he refrains from suggesting them absent a compelling reason, such as the parties' going in circles unproductively or reaching impasse. This way, he puts the responsibility for solutions squarely back in the parties' court.

19 *See supra* note 15.

Negotiations: goals and techniques

1. **Focusing**
2. **Clarifying**
3. **Asking open-ended questions**
4. **Paraphrasing**
5. **Reframing**
6. **Tracking and summarizing agreements**
7. **Reality testing**
8. **Allowing silence**

Caucus

In the negotiations stage, the mediator continues to help the parties focus on the future, moving from item to item on the agenda. At any time a party can request a caucus if she would like to speak privately with the mediator, and the mediator can suggest a caucus when negotiations seem to be going in circles or to reach impasse. What is said in caucus is not shared with the other party. Caucus provides an opportunity to check in with each party about how the process is going; to empathize, building trust; to discuss privately things the parties were hesitant to share in open session; to provide an opportunity for venting; to probe for underlying interests and concerns that may not have surfaced; to clarify priorities; to explore obstacles to settlement, helping parties clarify what they need in order to reach resolution; to reality test regarding what will happen if there is no agreement; to encourage empathy for the other party if appropriate; and to coach the parties on negotiations, helping them advocate successfully and effectively for themselves.

```
┌─────────────────────────────────────────────┐
│                                               │
│  Caucus: goals and techniques                 │
│                                               │
│         1.  Check in                          │
│         2.  Empathize, build trust            │
│         3.  Discuss privately[20]             │
│         4.  Allow venting                     │
│         5.  Probe for interests and concerns  │
│         6.  Clarify priorities                │
│         7.  Explore obstacles                 │
│         8.  Reality-test                      │
│         9.  Encourage empathy                 │
│         10. Coach                             │
│                                               │
└─────────────────────────────────────────────┘
```

---

20 A valid question could be raised about whether it is appropriate that a mediator mentioned the fact that a certain topic had been discussed in a caucus, even though not revealing any particular comments about that topic. The argument would be that merely learning that a given topic had been discussed with "the other side" could provide leverage to one party or a perceived loss of mediator neutrality, or both. Here, since the topic referred to by the mediator had been widely acknowledged in open session by both parties as a key issue for discussion, and since the Mediator mentioned that it had been discussed in not one, but both caucuses, and since nothing that either he or the parties said in caucus was shared, the potential concern was minimized.

Stage V: Resolution and Closure

In the last stage, the mediator clarifies the agreements the parties have reached. The mediator will raise potential contingencies that could arise, or "what ifs?," making sure that the parties have a plan for dealing with them. When parties have reached interim agreements at the end of each session or a final agreement at the end of the entire mediation, the mediator will act as a scribe, writing up those agreements so that they are specific and complete.

The Mediator clarifies the remaining agreements, including that Sherri will train Patty or another employee in customer service until Sara returns from maternity leave to resume the job, with Patty as backup.

When they return for the final session, Sherri and Jean will resolve the remaining items in dispute. The Mediator will help the parties finalize their written agreement, congratulate them on their effective cooperation, and encourage them to return to mediation should any problems arise in carrying out their agreement.

_____
_____
_____
_____
_____
_____
_____
_____
_____
_____
_____
_____
_____
_____
_____

```
Resolution and Closure: goals and techniques

    1.  Review and clarify agreements
    2.  Make a plan for contingencies
    3.  Write up agreements
    4.  Congratulate parties
    5.  Invite return to mediation if needed
```

_____

_____

_____

_____

_____

_____

_____

_____

_____

_____

_____

_____

_____

_____

_____

_____

_____

_____

_____

_____

About the Producers

Sue Ann Allen has twenty years experience as the Training Director for the Dispute Resolution Center of King County. In that capacity, she developed the volunteer training, and she oversees the training of the Center's volunteer court and community mediators. She designs courses for the public and tailors courses in conflict resolution skills and mediation to specific clients' needs, as well as providing training and supervision to the Dispute Resolution Center roster of trainers. Since becoming a mediator in 1984, she has served as a mediator for a wide variety of disputes in the work place, special education, faith-based groups, and the community. She is a former Board member of the Washington Mediation Association. Ms. Allen's extensive background in intercultural conflict resolution has led to a focus in that area. She has lived and worked in Europe, Asia, and Africa, as well as in diverse communities in the U.S. In addition to presenting at numerous regional and national conferences on conflict resolution, she has been honored to be selected as one of five trainers for a national collaborative effort to develop and conduct training through the National Association for Community Mediation. She is one of a small cadre of trainers and mediators for a national conflict resolution team for a faith-based, peacemaking initiative of the Community of Christ. Ms. Allen holds an undergraduate degree in secondary education from Central Michigan University and a graduate degree in community development from the University of Missouri-Columbia.

Melinda J. Branscomb is a tenured professor at the Seattle University School of Law, teaching courses in mediation, arbitration, collaborative law, negotiation, client counseling, torts, and labor and employment law. First trained as a mediator in 1989, she serves as a Special Education Mediator for the Washington public schools. She has mediated disputes for the Dispute Resolution Centers of King County, Thurston County, and Pierce County, and has served as a mentor-mediator in two mediator training programs. Prof. Branscomb helped teach Collaborative Problem Solving and Negotiation to the Guatemalan Human Rights Ombudsman's Office, and she taught Conflict Resolution and Community Development in Brazil. She is a frequent speaker on dispute resolution, employment law, and conflict avoidance in the workplace. Professor Branscomb coaches the S.U. teams in the ABA-sponsored law student competitions in Mediation Advocacy, Client Counseling, and Negotiation. As of the time this Manual went to press, S.U. teams have represented the Northwest Region at the national level five times in the last four years in these competitions. Professor Branscomb received her J.D. at the University of Tennessee School of Law (*Coif,* 1980, first in class) receiving a rare "Citation for Extraordinary Academic Achievement" from the law school faculty. She received her B.A., *cum laude* at Vanderbilt University, 1972.

The Dispute Resolution Center (DRC) **of King County** is the largest of the 20 community dispute resolution centers in Washington State and has provided training and services to the community for over 22 years. Dispute resolution centers have a unique structure that provides conflict resolution service to the community using highly-trained volunteer mediators as the primary services providers. The DRC offers an in-depth, rigorous mediation training program that includes a 2-year mentored practicum which produces highly-skilled mediators from all walks of life.

The DRC in King County uses a facilitative, interest-based style of mediation that helps people resolve disagreements with the help and facilitation of a neutral mediator. This style of mediation is confidential and is especially useful for disputes involving long-term relationships, such as neighbors, siblings, co-workers, or former spouses. Facilitative mediation leads to enforceable, voluntary agreements, yet it also allows for creative solutions. The safety and structure of the facilitative style can improve communication, promote understanding and strengthen relationships.

Seattle University School of Law, the largest and most diverse law school in the Pacific Northwest, is dedicated to the twin goals of academic excellence and education for justice. The School of Law is home to leading academic programs, including the top-ranked Legal Writing Program in the country, the Ronald A. Peterson Law Clinic, and distinguished institutes such as the Center on Global Justice, the Fred T. Korematsu Center for Law & Equality, the Center for Indian Law and Policy, the Access to Justice Institute, the Center for Global Justice, and the Center on Corporations, Law & Society. These programs and a superb faculty support the law school's mission to educate outstanding lawyers to be leaders *for a just and humane world*. The dispute resolution curriculum includes courses in general dispute resolution, client interviewing and counseling, negotiation, mediation, mediation advocacy, arbitration, collaborative law, and a law clinic in which students serve as mediators in employment discrimination cases filed with the Equal Employment Opportunity Commission (EEOC).

The school enrolls more than 1,000 students representing more than 250 undergraduate schools, drawn from the top third of the national law school applicant pool. The diversity of the student body encompasses age, life experience, and cultural heritage. The law school also is recognized nationally for its diverse faculty and welcoming environment. It is the only Washington law school with a part-time program geared to meet the needs of working professionals. The law school is accredited by the ABA and holds membership in the AALS. Students may pursue a J.D. or one of many joint degrees.

About the Mediator

Andrew Kidde, J.D., has 14 years of experience as a family law attorney and private mediator. He is the co-Manager for the Bellevue Neighborhood Mediation Program, where he trains and supervises volunteer mediators and conciliators who work on neighborhood disputes and other conflicts. He also conducts facilitations and public involvement workshops for the City of Bellevue Planning Department. Mr. Kidde is a certified mediator and former Board member of the Washington Mediation Association, and he has served as a mentor-mediator with the Dispute Resolution Center of King County. Mr. Kidde has extensive experience as a dispute resolution trainer in the Seattle area. He holds a master's degree in planning from Cornell University, 1988, and a J.D., *cum laude,* from Seattle University School of Law, 1992.

Post Script Regarding Multiple Sclerosis

The simulation is based on an actual conflict, with changes to party names and workplace. The "actor" in the video and the producers hope that the film educates viewers not only about mediation, but also about the challenges of MS. As in "Sherri's" situation, some disabilities initially may be difficult to identify, such as various auto-immune diseases, mental illness, physical limitations, and cognitive disorders. MS symptoms and severity vary greatly. Once the illness is diagnosed and discussed between the employer and employee, in many cases there are a variety of accommodations that can be implemented easily and inexpensively. Other needs can require more problem-solving.

Individuals with disabilities concerned about maintaining their employment or seeking new employment can contact your local or state Division of Vocational Rehabilitation (DVR) for assistance with assessment, compensatory strategies, equipment, planning, training and more. DVR offices are also a resource for employers wanting to learn more about reasonable accommodations. See also http://www.nationalmssociety.org.

About Multiple Sclerosis [21]

Multiple sclerosis, or MS, is a chronic, often disabling disease that attacks the central nervous system (CNS). Symptoms may be mild, such as numbness in the limbs, or severe, such as paralysis or loss of vision. The progress, severity, and symptoms of MS are unpredictable and vary from one person to another. Today, new treatments and advances in research are giving new hope to people affected by the disease. Most people with MS learn to cope with the disease and continue to lead satisfying, productive lives.

MS is Thought to be an Autoimmune Disease
The body's own defense system attacks myelin, the fatty substance that surrounds and protects the nerve fibers in the central nervous system. The damaged myelin forms scar tissue (sclerosis), which gives the disease its name. When any part of the myelin sheath or nerve fiber is damaged or destroyed, nerve impulses traveling to and from the brain and spinal cord are distorted or interrupted, producing the variety of symptoms.

---

21 From http://www.nationalmssociety.org/about-multiple-sclerosis/what-is-ms/index.aspx. © 2009 The National MS Society. Used with permission. For more information visit the National Multiple Sclerosis Society website at http://www.nationalmssociety.org.

The Four Courses of MS

People with MS can typically experience one of four disease courses, each of which might be mild, moderate, or severe.

- **Relapsing-Remitting MS.** People with this type of MS experience clearly defined attacks of worsening neurologic function. These attacks—which are called relapses, flare-ups, or exacerbations —are followed by partial or complete recovery periods (remissions), during which no disease progression occurs. Approximately 85% of people are initially diagnosed with relapsing-remitting MS.

- **Primary-Progressive MS.** This disease course is characterized by slowly worsening neurologic function from the beginning—with no distinct relapses or remissions. The rate of progression may vary over time, with occasional plateaus and temporary minor improvements. Approximately 10% of people are diagnosed with primary-progressive MS.

- **Secondary-Progressive MS.** Following an initial period of relapsing-remitting MS, many people develop a secondary-progressive disease course in which the disease worsens more steadily, with or without occasional flare-ups, remissions, or plateaus. Before the disease-modifying medications became available, approximately 50% of people with relapsing-remitting MS developed this form of the disease within 10 years.

- **Progressive-Relapsing MS.** In this relatively rare course of MS (5%), people experience steadily worsening disease from the beginning, but with clear attacks of worsening neurologic function along the way.

[N]o two people have exactly the same experience of MS .... And, it may not always be clear to the physician — at least right away — which course a person is experiencing.

Caucus Exercise Instructions

Using the transcript of the caucuses found in your MEDIATOR-TRAINEE AND STUDENT HANDBOOK for the DVD, *An Interest-based Mediation ... – A Narrated Mediator-training Video*, please answer the following questions.

A)   Find two points in the dialogue where each of these mediator techniques was demonstrated.

   1. Creating trust.

   2. Expressing empathy for a party.

   3. Facilitating empathy between the parties

   4. Clarifying

   5. Coaching a party about how to effectively negotiate

   6. Summarizing, or "tracking"

   7. Facilitating the parties' information-gathering.

   8. Paraphrasing facts or feelings that a party expressly or impliedly communicated.

B)   Find one additional place in each caucus where you, as Mediator, might have paraphrased the facts or feelings that the party expressed.

C)   Find one or more places where you might have used a question such as, "What would (does) that look like to you?," to help a party be more specific.

D)   How would you have responded to Sherri's expression of embarrassment about her emotional state at work before she was discharged?

An Interest-based Mediation - Caucus Exercise

4   Narrator:
5
6   In the negotiations stage, the mediator continues to help the parties focus on
7   the future, moving from item to item on the agenda. At any time a party can request
8   a caucus if she would like to speak privately with the mediator, and the mediator can
9   suggest a caucus when negotiations seem to be going in circles or to reach impasse.
10 What is said in caucus is not shared with the other party. Caucus provides an opportunity
11 to check in with each party about how the process is going; to empathize, building trust;
12 to discuss privately things the parties were hesitant to share in open session; to provide an
13 opportunity for venting; to probe for underlying interests and concerns that may not have
14 surfaced; to clarify priorities; to explore obstacles to settlement, helping parties clarify
15 what they need in order to reach resolution; to reality-test regarding what will happen if
16 there is no agreement; to encourage empathy for the other party if appropriate; and to
17 coach the parties on negotiations, helping them advocate successfully and effectively for
18 themselves.
    [...]

19   **Caucus with Jean**
20

21 Mediator: So Jean, I just want to remind you that this is a confidential meeting; I'm not
22   going to bring anything back to Sherri, unless you and I agree on that. I also
23   want to use this as a time to ask you some questions, maybe some tough
24   questions, and you have the freedom to answer them here in confidentiality.
25   A lot of what we are talking about here is the possibility of Sherri coming back
26   to work.
27
28 Jean: Right.
29
30 Mediator: You have indicated that that would be okay if she can fulfill the basic function
31   of the job.
32
    Jean: Yes.
33
34 Mediator: She's talked a fair amount about being accommodated for her disabilities
35   associated with the disease, and I'm wondering what your thoughts are on
36   that.
37
38 Jean: Well, I am open to Sherri coming back to her job, and we have been trying to
39   talk about some of the accommodations and haven't been able to make much
40   progress around it.
41
42 Mediator: Do you feel like your company is required to make accommodations?
43

1		
2	Jean:	Well, I have talked to our legal counsel about this somewhat, and it's kind of
3		questionable about this. We want to do the right thing. What I've been told
4		[is] it is a matter of degree of the accommodation.
5		
6	Mediator:	[You've been told] you have to make some accommodations.
7	Jean:	Perhaps, to be able to do the right thing legally, I don't know if we are required
8		to, but House Depot has always been committed to doing the right thing by
9		their employees, and we want to see if we can work something out, but we
10		can't be unreasonable in these accommodations.
11		
12	Mediator:	So you can make "reasonable" accommodations, however [that's] define[d]?
13		
14	Jean:	That's correct.
15		
16	Mediator:	I'm just wondering if it might be helpful to get some more information as part of
17		the process.
18	Jean:	Where would you suggest that I go?
19		
20	Mediator:	You know I don't know about that. Maybe we could ask Sherri. She might
21		have some leads, and maybe there are other places. Your legal department
22		might have some ideas as well.
23		
24	Jean:	But my concern, Andrew; I have a couple concerns here, and one is that Sherri
25		and I had a really strong relationship for nine plus years, and in the last several
26		months that relationship really deteriorated. And I'm concerned about if she
27		comes back, what kind of relationship we're going to have, 'cause I certainly
28		don't want to continue how the relationship has been in the most recent months,
29		and I'm very concerned about that. And the other concern I have is that if we
30		work out something today, what happens in three months if it's not working or
31		there are other kinds of symptoms that occur? What are the expectations that
32		she has, and as an employer what should I be expecting? I do know a little bit
33		about MS, and it can be a fairly dynamic illness, and my concern is just around
34		a dynamic illness and what could happen in the future.
35	Mediator:	Okay, okay.
36		
37	Jean:	But, again, I'm concerned about our working relationship. I think it's been
38		compromised. I haven't liked what I've had to do here. I didn't take any pleasure
39		in having to actually fire Sherri. I wish it could have been different. And I want
40		to set things up so I can succeed, she can succeed and the company can
41		succeed.
42		
43		

1	Mediator:	Okay.
2		
3	Jean:	And that is the kind of assurance I need in any agreement we are able to reach
4		out of this mediation process.
5		
6	Mediator:	Okay. So Jean I wanted to get a little more specific about these two concerns
7		of yours. The one being about the future and what's going to happen there and
8		the other being about your relationship.
9	Jean:	Right.
10		
11	Mediator:	In terms of this future one, I heard you say a couple of things that you think
12		might be important to resolve as part of that. One is exactly when Sherri is
13		planning on coming back, because that might affect how much of the customer
14		service work and so on and so forth. Maybe that's one thing we want to get
15		specific information about, is that right?
16		
17	Jean:	That could be helpful.
18	Mediator:	Okay then, moving on to the relationship. I guess I'm sort of wondering… you
19		had this strong relationship, it deteriorated. "What do you think the two of you
20		need in order to get to a better place?," I guess [is my question].
21		
22	Jean:	Well, I think there needs to be better communication, and I still don't understand,
23		when Sherri was experiencing all these things I've heard from her today in the
24		mediation, why she didn't tell me more about what was going on with her so I
25		had a better understanding of the difficulties that she was facing. So I think, to
26		be a little more forthcoming, and when I do ask, if she could tell me, that could
27		be very helpful. I don't want to pry, but at the same time if it is affecting what
28		she's doing at House Depot, I think it might be helpful for me to know that.
29		
30	Mediator:	So it sounds like you're looking for some communication about the specifics of
31		what's going on for her; that you need to know about stuff that is affecting her
32		work at House Depot, but you are not wanting to pry into her private life.
33	Jean:	Right, right.
34		
35	Mediator:	Well, that is very helpful. Well, what about her? What do you think she needs
36		in order to get to that better relationship?
37		
38	Jean:	Well, now that she's got this diagnosis of MS, if you look back to what's
39		happened the last several months, it comes into focus in a different way. If I
40		had known that, I think I would have been responding differently to what was
41		going on for her. So I imagine me saying something like that, that I'm very
42		sorry that she has this diagnosis, and if I had known I would have probably tried
43		

1	to act differently, and now that I do know, what we can do in the future to try to
2	work this out together.
3	
4	**Mediator:** Yeah, that seems important. Would you be willing to kind of lay that out with
5	her?
6	
7	**Jean:** I can try that.
8	**Mediator:** Okay, good. Well, I think that would be very helpful. Good, well, I think that is
9	all we need to do right now in the caucus, is there anything else you want to tell
10	me?
11	
12	**Jean:** I can't think of anything right now
13	
14	**Mediator:** Okay, great. Well, why don't you go on back out there, and I'll get Sherri.
15	
16	
17	**Caucus with Sherri**
18	**Mediator:** How are you feeling?
19	
20	**Sherri:** Kind of tired.
21	
22	**Mediator:** Yeah, I noticed you were looking a bit tired. Well, you just let me know if you
23	need any breaks. You know that's fine.
24	
25	**Sherri:** So did we get everything worked out?
26	
27	**Mediator:** Well, that is for the two of you to do, I guess, yes. So it sounds like you are
28	-- the two of you are -- really working on the idea that you could return to work
29	there. How does that feel to you?
30	**Sherri** I don't think we're quite there […] I feel used. They "chewed me up and spit me
31	out."
32	
33	**Mediator:** Boy, it seems like so many different factors coming into play here, doesn't it?
34	
35	**Sherri:** But the bottom line is for whatever reason, I still want to try it again and I want
36	them to give me that opportunity. And I think I deserve that.
37	
38	**Mediator:** It sounds like you'd be willing to apologize, and that you feel you're owed an
39	apology, too.
40	**Sherri:** Yeah, if it were sincere and mutual, you know. It's been a learning process
41	for all of us. In retrospect, I wish I would have done things differently. I wasn't
42	capable at the time, but I'm willing to own up to that if they are willing to own up
43	to their part of it and make some changes.

1 2 3 4 5 6 7	Mediator:	Okay, well I'd like to get us back together in a joint session, but before we do, I just want to recap what we have talked about, because I think it's very valuable. You talked about not wanting to do customer service, and one of the things that was underlying that was the difficulty you had controlling emotions. This is kind of an awkward thing because you don't want to talk about that, and yet, that is one of the core reasons you don't want to do it, that and the physical fatigue.
8 9 10 11 12 13	Sherri:	But I mean we don't even -- I would rather not talk about that. I'm just telling that to you because I kind of need to let it out. It's embarrassing. Even without that, just being called off the floor every two minutes to deal with customer complaints [was a problem]. Do you have to tell her that [MS caused me to have problems controlling emotions]?
14	Mediator:	I'm not going to tell her anything that you don't agree with....
15 16 17	Sherri:	It's just that we are having such an issue with power and control right now. I feel that makes me seem weak, and I don't want to mention it...
18 19	Mediator:	Yeah, I know.
20 21 22 23 24	Sherri:	But the physical aspect of the customer services, and how much it takes out of from my regular job I think is enough [to share]. I never said I wouldn't help train somebody, you know. I just said that I can't be doing this every time that somebody is not there to do it.
25 26 27 28 29 30 31 32	Mediator:	Well, that is an interesting thing. It might be a possibility worth proposing. Other accommodations that you talked about [were] the palm pilot -- Was that something that you were thinking they would provide for you to do the job? And proper instruction on this "Access" program? Possible assistance with the vendor tours? Getting around the facility? And there was another possibility that I wasn't sure if you wanted to pursue or not, which had to do with whether the employees at House Depot got some kind of education about working with [co-employees with] diseases. [...]
33 34	Sherri:	Yeah, I think that they should.
35 36 37 38 39 40 41 42 43	Mediator:	Okay. Let's bring Jean back in.

47

Made in the USA
Charleston, SC
25 September 2010